THE FIRE EATER'S LUNCHBREAK

THE FIRE EATER'S LUNCHBREAK

poems

November 10, 2007 – May 19, 2008

Daniel Abdal-Hayy Moore

The Ecstatic Exchange

2008

Philadelphia

For quotes any longer than those for critical articles and reviews,
contact:
The Ecstatic Exchange,
6470 Morris Park Road, Philadelphia, PA 19151-2403
email: abdalhayy@danielmoorepoetry.com

First Edition
ISBN: 978-0-6152-3628-5 (PAPER)
Published by *The Ecstatic Exchange*,
6470 Morris Park Road, Philadelphia, PA 19151-2403

Also available from The Ecstatic Exchange:
Knocking from Inside, poems by Tiel Aisha Ansari

Cover and text design by Abdallateef Whiteman
www.ianwhiteman.com
Cover collage by the author
Back cover photograph by Peter Sanders

بسم

To
Shaykh ibn al-Habib
(and the continuation of the Habibiyya)
Shaykh Bawa Muhaiyuddeen,
all shuyukh of instruction and ma'arifa
and
Baji Tayyaba Khanum
of the unsounded depths

The earth is not bereft
of Light

≈

CONTENTS

A NOTE ABOUT THE TITLE

WHAT DOES HAPPEN when we stop swallowing the flame, whatever it might be? This world, our own drudgery, our passions, low or high, that locus of our experience we call "*I*" – and take a break?

In what space, or in what time does that take place? Or are we ourselves turned inside-out in space and time when we let enter that momentary timelessness and spacelessness?

My first taste of such a "lunchbreak" was sitting in Buddhist Zazen with Sensei Shunryu Suzuki in San Francisco in the 60s. Facing the wall. Letting the flames subside. Not quenching them completely, but sitting near them for the first time without getting totally fried, letting them flitter across the mental horizon and fade.

Upon entering Islam in a Sufi Tariqat in 1970, the Shadhiliyya of Morocco with Qutb Shaykh Muhammad ibn al-Habib, I found a world where the lunchbreak was well established, obviously with the Master and with many of his venerable disciples. They seemed dimensionally free of the world's entanglements while still within its actions, reactions and compassions. *What a Paradise on earth!* How sweet to be an effective actor in the human transaction, giving and taking, being even congenial or grumpy (yes even grumpy, like the Zen Master who said, "*Before I became enlightened I was miserable, and after I was enlightened I was as miserable as ever!*") but within the almost visible globe of God's unique and constantly beneficent influence, and deeply within the spirit of the ever-present and loving stewardship of the Prophet Muhammad, peace be upon him, His Prophet and Messenger.

There's a Sufi text by Shaykh ibn 'Ata Illah whose title I've always loved: *The Giving Up of the Management of Your Affairs.* Neat trick! But somehow that's also the key to the present title, and God willing to something of the poems this book contains.

For thirty years I have been talking to God and people thought I was talking to them.

—ABBAAS IBN ʿISAAM
(contemporary of Shaykh Junayd)

You never have to change anything you got up in the middle of the night to write.

SAUL BELLOW, American author

I SEVERAL RAINBOWS

Several rainbows from various things
that fly in great arcs in all directions
illuminating walls and floors with their

spectral harmony their almost audible
scales of color beyond the visible

wake up denizens of another universe
to intense blue daylight

11/10

2 CELEBRITY PORTRAITS

A golden coach comes to a stop and
out steps Marie Antoinette who
has the head of a squirrel

Lucretia Borgia looks out over his
exquisite Venetian lace collar and
he is a ferret

Lord Byron hops across the drawing room to
read us his new Don Juan Cantos
and wrinkle his pink nose and
scratch his long white ears

11/11

3 ANGEL OF DEATH IN GOLD LAMÉ

The angel of death has on a gold lamé
tunic wings tucked under and sparkly

cloche hat and neon multicolored skirts
that billow like waterfalls in tropical sunlight

in some grotto'd hideaway and sets out to the
hilarity of the other angels in their

general somber or invisible attire
slapping non-existent knees that make

sonic booms and various aurora borealises of
high celestial music heard only faintly

by even the saintliest of mortals

"I have to go in a way they'll recognize"
Azrael says to the others and

slips between clouds only to
appear to a select few at a

New York club just before closing time
fitting in perfectly and unseen except by the

new members of God's wedding guest list

surprised at how much better the next world is
both than they'd previously thought as well as

where they had spent their entire lives so
dutifully being

11/18

4 MEN AND WOMEN

That men have a little spout
and women a little trough

makes some people scream and shout
and others shuffle and cough

11/21

5 STORY ABOUT A TIGER

There's a story about a tiger I just can't remember
They crowded around to try to dismember

her and each separate part then sprang into life
as a *separate* tiger – they yelled *run for your life!*

11/22

6 SCIENTIFIC PHENOMENON

These tidal waves that wipe out
entire villages

Is it the wrath of God or just some
scientific phenomenon?

But isn't God also
a scientific phenomenon?

11/22

7 MAJESTIC BY THAT MUCH MORE

The incredulousness of the crowd
can't undermine the elegance of certitude

When certitude's like a sunny hillside
where contented sheep and goats graze

and the shepherd's asleep under a tree

"*Let them roar their incomprehension*"
says the sharp rabbit looking over a slope

a blade of grass half hanging out its mouth
down at the writhing mass

Nothing can be taken from God's Grandeur
that doesn't make it majestic by that much more

11/24

8 AWAY FROM HOME

We're visiting our two sons in Zurich and London

but I miss the wintry sunlight coming through our

dining room window ferns in Philadelphia

11/24

9 KNOT OF GOLD

The Prophet took people of abject poverty
and strewed rubies at their feet

There was no glass in the Prophet's windows
for any brick to break

In each heart he ties a knot of gold
whose two ends make eternity's

radiant reclining figure eight
gazed upon by God

We can stand in the door he made in
our being or stride through it into God's

Presence

The Prophet never rode out on his she camel
but that they longed for his return

11/24

10 GATE

Death's not a place nor a state
but a gate

And the embers we leave behind
are cold and dead

I sit among the living to write this
on the edge of my marital bed

11/24

11 SECRETS

Is she whispering state secrets to me
or deep wisdom from beneath God's loftiest Throne

or is she just ever so lightly and softly and even
melodiously snoring?

11/24

12 JOY OF THE PHOENIX

The joy of the Phoenix must be in its burning
and the moment that out of its ashes it

spreads its ancient wings again and rises
with not a single ash flake unaccounted for

And the ash was formless the moment before
not one moment of further possible burning

Not one glimmer of red ember furtively radiant
out of the bland neutrality of ash

A new vigor of resplendent Phoenix making
air waves of rainbow color stutter off its flight

And yet the single heartbeat of these
transformations doesn't come from Phoenix

Allah's purpose for metamorphosis and origination
propels not only burning and ash-making

but reconstitution and flight for a new destination
with its eyes clear as beacons looking for

Phoenix prey whose prayer is constant
renewal and perpetual divine nearness

11/25

13 THE WINE WE LOVE

The wine we love is the wine of the spirit
The wine we avoid is the wine of the body

Though the wine of the body lead to spiritual bliss
its dregs and bitters are magical temptation

Shattering the glass is the way to the pure wine
though the glass itself is the wine and the

wine itself the glass
and the lips that sip are also the blesséd drink

that we think by simply sipping we'll be
able to drink

And we drown in the world of what is
always drunkenly around us

whose otherworldly bubbles of light always
drunkenly surround us

11/25

14 SIGNATURE POEM

My wife asks what will be my
signature poem my *Mathnawi* my *Howl* my

Tyger Tyger

What painting of Picasso's is his signature painting?
Guernica is the one that brings together

all his powers but it is simply
a door to all his other work

And *Tyger Tyger* is a door to the rest and
best of Blake

I continue to write to find that poem

I write to get it right

11/25

15 BILLOWING SHEETS OF SUNLIGHT

Billowing sheets of sunlight in the darkness

Billowing sheets of sunlight in the darkness

Billowing sheets of sunlight in the darkness

Billowing sheets of sunlight in the darkness

11/25

16 ANNOUNCEMENT

The announcement takes place on a celestial bullhorn of
cerulean crystal from a

Matterhorn peak so snow-blown it's become immaterial or
was immaterial from time immemorial

And the sound so pure a blast of vivacity its
sonic boom keeps every spine tingling with its

otherworldly message traveling upright or horizontal in
this world across earth's curve or aloft arc floating

above or afloat below sound's watery curlicue

Each throb comes from it each ding dong bell each
swell of pride in ant or bee or swallow's

buoyant looping like pairs of scissors in a twilit
pewter sky across eternity

And it's the annunciation of life and
death from the selfsame horn and with the

selfsame vibrational timbres that make
the sun both shine its volatile gold and

turn as purple as a bruise
when day is done

11/26

17 EVERYONE BUT GOD

> *Heard melodies are sweet, but those unheard*
> *Are sweeter* — KEATS

Given names are indications
but unpronounced names within them
reverberate in secret forests where
white egrets rise like geysers into
clear air

A lover's glance is a deep musical chord
held on a ventricular piano
but God's glance once given transforms
the beloved into a full-bodied choir
that wakes birds in distant trees and
spins stars in black skies

Some actions withheld in a realm of silence
might stop floods or reverse
wars bring the dead
back to life or send some staggering into
thirsty deserts searching for their lost souls

Our existence is an enigma to
everyone but God

11/27

18 VERY TINY HORSE

A very tiny horse neighs
and the sun comes up like thunder

A waterfall ceases falling
revealing a stone wall underneath

Swift birds fly in the direction of their intention
returning to their origin with each
wingbeat forward

Has even one page been turned
or one truth revealed?

No one should worry too much when their
life is over
that their life is over

A very tiny horse neighs
and the sun comes up like thunder

11/28

19 A PROMISE

An old man looked at himself in a mirror
and saw a young man become old

He thought he could just hop away like a
cricket and join the other forest dwellers

There's a star for each one of us
in a heaven ordained for each of us alone

Getting there is half the battle
arriving there is the gift of love

I once saw a man on a bicycle
ride through a doorway into sunlight

He's gone from young to old
and old to young in a second

The universe turns with majesty
around a center that is nowhere

You can hear the dawn lifting
its million tiny feet

God has made a promise
we've been made to fulfill

11/28

20 BATHED IN SILVER

At the house of strangers
the host is also the guest

A blue moon sinks below the hillside
leaving everything in darkness

Moving through the night is one way of
finding out who you are

This bridge or that bridge is always a question
with no single answer

One step takes you further
one step brings you closer

Verification comes when you least expect it
from an intimate unforeseen quarter

Only shadowless beings can indicate
the direction to be taken

Once a house is entered
the only exit's a doorway

When the moon comes up
everything's bathed in silver

11/28

21 A QUANDARY OF GORGEOUS SONG

The Prophet Muhammad's arrived again
with an entourage of saints

Birds are flying in such a way
the sky is streaked with gold

He settles down to a cool murmur
and everywhere rivers flow

None of our words are anything
but his messages of silver

Their light is like a thousand universes
with a thousand burning suns

Once seen he can't be forgotten
Once heard he can't be ignored

Beauty denied is
justice thrown down a well

Justice denied is
beauty left bleeding on the road

He's left us with ourselves at last
in a quandary of gorgeous song

11/28

22 ONE WHITE HAIR

Death is a white hair that lands on our
lapel that can't be returned to our head

Once having left our native land
how can we return?

Once we're cut off from our source
how can we find our way again?

Unperturbed by events that showed us
death's horrid doorways

the white hair that lands on our lapel
lies silent and still

Once we move off from our starting place
we're sure to arrive where we've never been before

Only God can catch us with sure hands
and bathe us in sudsy waters

The eyes' windows shut down at death
and His windows open

The heart's windows are never closed
here or there

One hair alone is enough to show us –
Take heed of that falling hair!

11/28

23 THE TEACHERS

A preposterous number of jewels are laid at our feet
from the teachings of the great teachers

Some galaxies turn in neon swirls around
incandescent centers

Some like giant plates of light stretch out
across their allotted space in infrared glory

Some behind others or behind black holes or
somehow obscured we can't see at all

God's scattered them in perfect proportions and
wisdom's symmetry even lopsidedly in space

Each one speaks its own language
known by the stardust particles of our inner ear

Nothing's left to chance in this most
liberal of existences

Nothing in creation's left out
of His magnificent control

Each breath is an internalized text clarified
by the lung's natural expansions and contractions

The teachers arrive one by one or all in a crowd
but their voice is one and their message is one

The sphinx's face looks out across the dark
with its enigmatic smile

But behind each face is the Prophet's face
and behind his face is God's

11/29
(*after Shaykh Abu Bakr's*
evening discourse)

24 BABY'S CRY IN THE NIGHT

for Mukhtar and Soraya

When a baby wakes up in the middle of the night
making cries like the ripping of wood and water

you can almost see the commotion of angels
in a vortex above her in the blackness

The entire village is asleep and only
wolves prowling with incandescent eyes

through the sleeping streets might hear her
among the living creatures

She's in pre-speech and this is her only
articulation almost forming later words

these cries might ignite into being

She stops to listen for a reply

The mother wide awake waits for her
to find the answer for herself

And when she finally falls back to
sleep she almost seems to have found it

11/30

25 TALE OF THE FOX AND THE EGG

It is better to be used than to be wasted

— MALIKA MOORE

An egg sat by the side of the road
and called out for someone to

come along and break it

(*I'm writing this on a flight from
London to Philadelphia so I can't be*

held to the veracity of this one)

Below us in the dark of the Atlantic is a
fabulous palace built of incandescent

coral

Wise and elegant fish swim in and out of its
gigantic bubbling rooms

There's a network of Utopian palaces
in the depths of the sea no man or

woman has seen and lived to tell

Only the word "*Peace*" is heard resounding
through its resplendent echoless halls

A fox who hadn't yet breakfasted
came along and sat opposite the egg

"*Why would you want to be a broken egg?*"
though his hunger was steadily increasing

The egg confronted with the hungry fox
suddenly became a perfect oval of silence

Everything has a purpose in God's world
and nothing is by accident

Though the undersea palaces may not exist
the idea of them is enticing

The fox had a gorgeous red tail
that he wrapped around his forepaws

The egg had no tail nor any features at all
but its egg shape and of course

a delicious interior

I have no idea where this poem is
going nor why it arrived at this moment in the

first place

(*My wife just asked to be let out of her seat
and will be back any minute*)

The airplane rocks gently back and forth
as it bravely crawls through the night

We're all going somewhere and it had
better be Paradise rather than nowhere

or Hell

"*If I'm broken I may be liberated*"
"*But if you're broken you may get eaten!*"

"*I'll take that chance fox rather than
sit here forever*"

This poem is all very tenuous yet it
has a strange and curious reality

(*My wife came back and nearly innocently
derailed my train of concentration*

It seems to take place almost without me
except I have to hold tight to its motions)

Now fox and egg and palaces undersea
are about to dissolve away completely

I think both fox and egg achieved their desire
though one was spiritual and the other

nutritional

Everything serves as something for someone
God is everywhere Sovereign over all

12/1

26 ALONE IN THE ALONE

All the verticals and horizontals in the world
line up to give the impression of appreciable form

Without their busily leaping and
dancing in the stillness of space each
moment all would be amorphously
formless and unable to project its
precise individual meaning

This table that chair that rose that
passing impression or attitude have
all geometrically arrived as the result of
gazillions of commands from God's
incalculable Throne

utterly gorgeous and powerful in its
magnificent singularity dear God

to right in front of our faces
from His pure Face alone
in The Alone

12/3

27 BOAT

A boat's pushing out to sea
and everyone's in it

There are no stragglers
nor is anyone missing

I've never been here before

12/3

28 GRENDEL

Will the Grendel of nightmare come and

slaughter us in our sleep?

Is that what we fear?

12/3

29 HIS HIGH COMMAND

His High Command
and an ant's vibrating antenna

The horrors of war
and a newborn's uncurling fingers

Flash floods
and a dry riverbed gurgling

The heart alone
and entire humanity's pulse beat

The earth turns
and the universe swims through space

One galaxy among millions
and the tear drop of His High Command

Nothing at all
and the magnificent multitudes

12/4

30 SIZE OF THE UNIVERSE

Is the universe the size of a pinprick in vellum
exquisite in its minuteness though we

can't tell the difference?
God alone knows

Or is it the dimensions of a magnificent vastness
whose edges continue to extend as soon as

they're reached?
God alone knows

Or neither or both at the same time
and we may not know which

until we become the size of a pinprick in vellum
or the dimensions of a magnificent vastness

whose edges continue to extend
as soon as they're reached

God alone knows

12/6

31 DIALOG

A whale said to a minnow *"I see you
still think you're the king of the world"*

The minnow said to the whale *"I can't get
back far enough to have a fair perspective"*

The ocean is more than a drop in the bucket
whose surfs beat distant and exotic shores

Outer space photographs of the earth's globe
show them somehow holding firm

Their waters don't fly off into space
leaving their basins dry their whales gasping

The earth's in space the way the
whales are in the sea

confident of their resiliency

While we're minnows to God's Supremacy

12/6

32 BIG NAKED BODY

We are a big naked body from head to toe
subject to electrical impulses from within

If a horse's head appears at your right shoulder
don't be afraid it's just a spirit come to be

comforted or to bless

Rainbow bridges everywhere invite our
expulsion from this place but their time may never come
or they may simply waver there in the ether

The sound of rushing water is a comfort
and little children throwing themselves into
its bifurcating streams a radiant bliss

When we stand up our heads enter heaven
when we're horizontal the voices of angels
sustain us

No hurt too deep cannot be assuaged
by the light of a merciful puzzle

Nothing confounds us more often and more deeply than the
endless sea of mercy we find ourselves in
and no shore anywhere in sight

Alive may be the only state we know
but death is the ingredient most
conducive to the soul's self knowledge

Its shadow crosses our path alerting us
to its wonders and life and death curl into
each other like two sides of a
falling leaf that lands upright at our
feet when we least expect it

Whenever we stand up to go anywhere
the whole universe changes position

Whether or not we hear them the near
singing of angels animates our thoughts

A light moves among us searching for our hearts
and blinks successfully into the
nutrients of our heartbeats

The white horse that appears at your side
has never been ridden before but its
nature is docile and its capacity for
galloping tireless

Outer space turns out to be
nearer to us than we know

Its map shouldn't be hard to find
in expectation's benevolence
of mind

12/9

33 GOD'S ELEGANT LONG-DISTANCE SWIMMERS

Death wears a grin we can't fathom
life is more than a short spasm

Death stops at a house down the street
"Life do your stuff" says heart to feet

Death sits down at the next table
It got Lana Turner and Betty Grable!

Life takes a long walk humming to itself
Knowing it'll never read all the books on its shelf

Death treads water in the kiddie pool
Life shuts its eyes and goes to school

These parallels could go on indefinitely
though life has an end we can't foresee

A strong golden glow up ahead shimmers
for all God's elegant long-distance swimmers

12/13

To write a secret book he dips his secret
pen into the center of a pearl

and its tip touches distant galaxies

He catches the scent of the Prophet's hair from Konya
and the drip of it runs down the stem of his

heart's rose

Of course there are white stallions
running along the margins of the sea

who turn into sea foam

And an arctic sun at midnight
to whose magnetic pull our blood turns

singing indescribable melodies

And only those can hear his song who were
there at its inception

which is everyone

And of course the paper his secret book is
written on becomes the flight of an albatross

in a slant of raw sunlight

And as soon as it's written it's no longer
a secret

And when it's no longer a secret
the entire world becomes silent

and all the planets turn in their
whistling courses

and our heartbeats follow them

12/14

35 GLORY IN THE DARKNESS

"Glory in the darkness" says the clock on the wall
"as your ship goes out through the ice"

"But the walls and floors obstruct us"
sing off-register voices from emptiness

"Charge inside lightning that dances at midnight"
calls the grass out the window still damp from dew

"Nowhere is without His activating Grace"
screams the fire truck siren hurrying down the street

Then the abiding silence laps back like surf
and the small noises pick themselves out of it again

The hand that writes this is as mortal as a moth
though in the script that flows are glimmers of first light

All our hearts are poised on eternity's picket fence
watching both sides at once for signs and wonders

But to stand in the darkness with arms outstretched
is the ant's way of glorying in the all-encroaching grandeur

And love's way of holding us close to its mouth
to hear its single heartbeat reverberate past death

12/19

36 IF I THINK

If I think I may never
write another poem

a thimbleful of ash might serve me

And when I look down into it
a vast canyon opens up

into the heart of the world

12/28

37 ACROSS AND ACROSS

For Baji

The ocean sank to its knees and started sobbing
though no one saw anything out of the ordinary

It's what the ocean is always doing most
people thought *sighing and sobbing and*

throwing itself against its shores
then pulling back and doing it all over again

"*I have everything inside me*" it stuttered between sobs
"*the tiniest creatures alive some even just one atom big*

deep down dead things as well as giant
eyes and hearts always on the lookout
endlessly meandering

The most complex thoughts as well as
utter placid thoughtlessness in flat places under the sun

I can't fit inside a single shell
but I can imagine I can
one spiral and I'm caught in sweet containment

I know my Lord loves me
out in the far reaches as well as the near

His Face shimmers down on my uneven surfaces
and all I need do is reflect it back to Him"

The engine of the sea was roaring as usual
its perpetual motion purred in its usual mode

What was its complaint? It had its
knowledge at its zillion sizzling fingertips

Yet it could be heard even from inland windows
sobbing and sighing without cease all night and day

It's original hurt or its original harboring?

Its boundaried outlandishness or its
one-pointed ocean song sung beyond doomsday?

It sobbed and sighed and stuttered between sighs
but no one thought there was anything unusual in its

usual *shush* and *reshush*
the shushing language God gave it to slide in silence

across in
always across in

across and across in

12/28

38 APOTHECARY JARS

Apothecary jars on shelves of burnished silver
beakers filled with smoke gurgling in the dark

Something must be brewing from these nefarious ingredients
shamans in the depths of shadowy forests might use

Bits of waxed thread amber in its gum form
shedding lovely golden glows on the proceedings

Cotton dipped in liquid light then dabbed on clean surfaces
(I'm not even sure what these various things are for)

Maybe buried deep in Bavaria mountain fastnesses
these laboratories exploding sometimes with transformations

Their innocent practitioners having to stand back suddenly
while a whole new creation forms before their eyes

Not a mote or motion goes by without God's knowledge
every shred of evidence left behind or in eternity

Each new combination of antiquated materials
that opens its infant eyes on this rapidly passing world

Suddenly it's quiet in the alchemist's environment
everything assumes a uniform pewter sheen

Rumblings are heard from distant deep volcanoes
even straight pins on the floor begin to vibrate

The sky leans lower and the earth strains up to meet it
there's suddenly an unearthly but inclusive coming together

Unseen world and seen world embrace in broad daylight
an audible whisper of intelligible phrases is clearly heard

This poem tumbles into being with all its shortcomings
the way a whirling dervish solemnly steps onto the floor

and takes its joy and gnosis by simply circulating
where before there'd been nothing but the usual equilibrium

It all takes place in silence
and returns there when it's done

New windows are opened
where before there'd been none

                                        12/28

39 LADDERS

for John Heron

Some ladders go up some ladders
go down

It's true! Of course all ladders intrinsically
go both ways

both up *and* down
though we prop one up to climb out of

somewhere or
put one down to climb down into somewhere

But in both cases we'd climb back down or
back up unless we can keep

going at the level we've climbed up or
down to without needing to return

The tall wind-blasted fairy-castle caves at
Capadoccia in Turkey have ladders going way up

then precariously down

We had to climb down to prophet Daniel's
supposed tomb on *Prophet Daniel Street* in Alexandria

then had to clamber precariously up

It all depends where we begin
down or up and where we need to go

up or down

Oh and take a ladder when you leave this poem
would you?

Climb up there and see if
anyone's listening?

12/29

40 THE ROTATIONAL CIRCUMFERENCE OF THINGS

A whale passed in the depths of the sea
in the shape of a school bus

But instead of children's faces at the window
a row of barnacles glimmered on its sides

An ant wore a leaf costume one day to
see if it could confound the others

One ant came upon it and hoisted it in its
mandibles light as any other leaf

(The protest from the other ant is
not recorded but they don't seem to make

noticeable noise so he was
presumably carried off in silence)

Once a rock longed to be on the other side of a
road near a very nicely shaped rock that

attracted its very robust rock nature but it was a
rock and had a clear understanding of its stationary position

so it concentrated all the magnetic force inside it
and one day a cow kicked it across the road

to its desired location next to the
other rock and they've been together ever since

Things are always shivering and shaking in the real world
and changing places as well as identities

Nothing remains the same for long though it
may take millenniums to be noticeable in

any measurable way

The earth isn't as flat as it seems it seems
but its rondure is deceptive as we're

all neighbors of one another from
wherever we are to the topmost and bottommost of the globe

A nice thought if you consider that caribou and kangaroos have been
running our governments for decades

though they may seem normal loping or hopping off in their natty
suits and ties after they've passed some

particularly timely legislation

Only the Creator can account for all the
minute calibrations in His creation

Or one of His saintly ones for whom
only His Face alone has any abiding reality

that lasts longer than an inhalation
upon whose stream all our concerns float like

soap bubbles formed around nothingness
gone almost before they've formed

in the torrential rotational
circumference of things

12/30

41 FRESH TOAD

You may be learned in the sciences
but are you learned in the brush

that sweeps the dust out
or the match that burns the dross?

A goose came out to inspect the project
and nip my heels

I hadn't seen a rainbow in days
and here I was collecting them

You put down your name on the
roster of the willing and the sacrificed

but can you part with one
hair of your head or chin or one

facial expression that has
fallen into disuse?

The steep side went down a very long way
and suddenly

but the expanse below was of a beautiful
emerald green as lush a valley as

these eyes had ever seen

You've come to this point and
here you'll stay for millennia

unless the snail shell on your back
gets jettisoned and the

pictures in your parlor turn to flame

I sometimes think this far is far enough
and am content with the reapings

Sometimes I realize my exuberance
isn't resonant enough and should be

more content with everything as it is

And the earth turns just as rapidly
and the birds make their last

flurries against the sunset before
bedding down

But the stern face in the window
gave no indication this was the

desired answer to the unanswerable
question

and looked on with the same
stern look as before

"I wouldn't' go anywhere by yourself
if I were you"

it was known to be fond of saying
whenever anyone came before it

The roses blew from east to west
and our hearts from west to east

but the waters higher than the rest
continue to flow down

The wolf waits outside the door
with bated breath

Do we have a bone to give it
or a fresh toad?

1/1

42 DEEP DOWN INTO THINGS

We're not here very long

so while we're here
we might as well try to get

deep down into things

1/2

43 DEATH IS COMING

Death is coming
and we're going to have a

lawn party
though it be winter

I'm going to wear my hat

The wheels of earth are
revolving with a grinding sound

I can make out death's face
in the mist

How can I believe it
with light all around?

Not even a little door
is needed that's how fully

dimensional I feel and
green shoots growing in space

everywhere at once
in the winter chill

1/4

44 IF OUR MOUTHS

If our mouths were like the flight of birds
gathering and scattering

with light-glints splattering from the
undersides of our wings

and we alighted easily from branch to branch
dipping into a water trough from time to time

and as easily sang our own songs to
split the air into staves of audible music

Or if our speech were a soft hand on a hot brow
or what came from our tongues was always
a dark confection wrapped in silence

as if from a secret treasure house of
unraveling stories whose arcs in space
hang curtains of aurora borealis
from vision to vision and from eye to eye

and if our throats were hallowed tabernacles
of deep organ pipes from underground caverns
where only a single water drop drips with its

succinct and perfect ping of destination

Or the movement of herds across savannas
our tongues against our teeth their hoof beats as they
run to safer ground by a black lake
under sunlight

and every word we uttered were pure coin
backed by true gold and sparkling silver

and we could move through the
mutual waterfalls of our speech

becoming wisdom-drenched and
splattered with love's delight...

1/5

45 ONE MORE WORD

How can we add one more word to it
one more syllable one more

breath to what is already at its
peak of perfection its absolute facets of

the entire crystal reflecting everything
perfectly with no extra membrane

even one smudge of murkiness or
shadow even one throat-clearing

pause of doubt it's so airtight and so
completely expressed the trillions of

gazillions of perfect bees aswarm or
inspecting the insides of flowers

and the quadrazillions of flowers themselves on
their nocturnal hillsides also

holding their breath so perfectly
there in their *thereness* each

petal-tip perfect
each movement on earth the

size of Gibraltar in a seismic seizure
of even one nano-micro-meter of

shift ever so slightly also affecting
nothing so much as the totally endearing

nothingness that is
within which in silence we

call out to Allah lips unable to actually
add one more word to it in its

monumental simplicity that inadequate
word of which is also actually

too much it's all simply
Allah

1/11

46 PRESIDENTIAL CANDIDATE

A little turquoise beetle with red dots on it
wanted to become president

It wandered for days over the front page of
a newspaper on the road reading the news

memorizing the dates and places and other
candidates' names and their platforms

It nearly got crushed but managed to avoid
a truck tire that got loose from its hub

But the newspaper was ruined
so the little beetle set its jaw with determination

and set out as well for a more densely populated area
to try out its campaign

It came across a rotting rat carcass filled with
maggots and a few ants and cleared its

little throat and began speaking
"*My fellow Americans*" it squeaked in High Beetle

They all just kept lunching
A few maggots seemed interested but the ants

couldn't be bothered
Yet our beetle maintained its dignity and

spoke for an hour about the plight of insects and
how they outnumber all other creatures on earth and

therefore should look to their rights and
responsibilities and elect him as their most qualified candidate

As twilight descended the little turquoise beetle with
red dots on it found itself poignantly

closing its speech with tears of compassion in
its eyes to the gaping bone structure of a

rat carcass with its sharp and prominent incisors
gleaming in the last of the day's dwindling light

1/12

47 LAKE ON A HILL

Is a lake on a hill closer to God than a
lake on a plain with its

bright reflective waters?

Is the dial on the watch of a saint
closer to true time than the

dials of the rest of us?

Is the night longer or shorter for
one who believes or one who disbelieves

that at the farthest end of it a glorious oasis arises?

(Slender palm trees there bend and tremble in the
sweetest wind)

Is the voice of the Beloved
licked inside our ears

clearer than our own voice and the
voices of others on the outside?

Is outside any different from
inside in God's Eyes?

1/15

48 DOORKNOB

There's a doorknob that
gleams like the moon

and when you open the door
you're bathed in moonlight

A giraffe with a short neck
who sits by you as you

lunch

A prairie of pink grass
blades blowing in one direction

and a sky that fills with water
like a sink

silvery and bright

Enter with exuberance and caution
and the trees will embrace you with their

mossy arms

The boats of the spaces between trees
will rock you to your destination

and none of this is possible
without God's elemental regiments of

perfection

perfect in every tendril and drop
whose sound right now

dazzles my innermost ears

purple in the morning light

1/17

49 HORSES

No corral could keep the horses in
on Rathsberger's farm

The higher the fences the higher they'd
soar over the tops of them

They electrified the fences but it only made
the horses' leaps that much more graceful

They put them in small enclosures
and almost by miracle they'd find them

next morning dotting the long green hillsides
as if they were wild

These horses were not that exceptional
two or three white ones some sorrel a

roan or two then blacks and browns
a whole assorted gamut of horses

By day docile and sweet
by night sleek and aloft in spaces

none but the horses themselves
could fathom

But if you looked into their eyes
their endlessly deep lake upon black lake of

tranquility eyes you'd know more than
sheer statistics could tell you

about these celestial earthlings
none with visible wings

as normal as you or me
except that no corral could

ever keep them in

Hearts on fire

Eyes ablaze

God's horses

1/18

50 LITTLE SOLDIERS

Death stands by a diagnosis
waiting for a nod

which is something that can
only be given by God

One day an ache or pain
proves to be fatal

The angel of death will
stand just inside the gate he'll

beckon with one finger or
lower a wing

and behind him we'll hear
clouds begin to sing

And over the vast expanse of the
hours of our life

will fall the shadow of a
net to keep each moment safe

and they'll add up to what
we'll bring on that fateful day

to hear the words of a reprieve
only God can say

though we long to hear them
in the flush of life

our heartbeats like little soldiers
falling over the cliff

of life and death to float
on an updraft of light

that would blind anyone
with normal sight

as our breaths dissolve
into His aerial Grace

that beams upon us
with His silent Face

1/20

51 THE DRUNKEN SOLDIER

The drunken soldier broke down
the wrong door

Inside was a circle of saints
lifted off the ground

To the sound of gunfire
a really supernal yellow light
shone round them

His jaw dropped
and his heart stopped

In the dark of the room
he saw his place

At the cost of so much blood
so little decency

The saints admitted him
to their convocation

The rest of the world went
dizzily into the background

The rest of the war popped in his
ears like distant fireworks

The young soldier
lifted off the ground

Suddenly his age didn't prevent him
from becoming ancient

The hearts in that room
were made of bronze and
royal copper

In their burnished surfaces
the Face of God shone resplendently

The drunken soldier
broke down the wrong door

Inside was a family of saints
huddled together

In the death of decency
so much bloodshed

The circle of saints
admitted him to their company

The drunken soldier
broke down the wrong door

Inside they
broke bread

1/22

52 IT'S A MARVEL

It's a marvel we have any life at all
with the way we are

That we breathe at the end of the day
and take it up again at the
beginning of a new one though we've been
breathing all along
through the long night

whose moon is a white owl flying through a belfry
with a mouse in its mouth

heading for the boats ready to circumnavigate
the globe

What we've done on the planet is a scandal
rivers of blood and heads and hearts
lopped off

It's a miracle we're still here
putting a smiley face on it all
floating downstream through the red waters

A shout only echoes so far
sobs only carry on so long

The Merciful One certainly is merciful
but we should count on our own mercy
to pull it through
reflective of its inner ardor

Nowhere do we see a shudder
like the one we put through creation
by the way we are

After natural disaster comes utter silence
birds in the air singing above wreckage

But when our rampages are done
the sound of sawing and the sobbing of
bones louder than Victoria Falls in their
deafening roar

Gratitude doesn't even begin to cover
what we should be feeling
for the utter marvel we have any life at all
with the way we are here

endlessly

in order to savor the favor

1/29

53 MOUSE FEET

Teeny-tiny mouse feet run along my ceiling
in rapidly fluttery pitty-pats

God's dimension is so vast all the
ticking clocks face sideways

There's a sound in the universe so pure
only one of us can hear it

Way at the end there
that silhouette of someone

standing against the moon

When you lift pen to paper
the savannah floods with light

If we're only visiting for a short time
will our echoes elongate behind us?

There's a shack blown down by the wind
all its nails shrieking

When the scrolls are unrolled
everything will come clear

Will we be there?
(*There go those mouse feet again above me*

Is he in such a hurry
to find my mousetrap?

If he pokes far enough in
he won't be able to get out

I let them loose in the woods
at the end of our street

Little tiny creatures
with delicate finger-and-toe nailed feet)

1/30

54 LIKE *THIS* DEATH!

Death you funny old fogy
Death you amorous adolescent
ivy in your hair

Death you ring around the tub
Death you perfect slick icicle

Death you pork rind on sizzling bun
Death you bus out of control in the Andes

Death you pop-goes-the-weasel
Death you swansong in full moonlight

Death you full swoon on an Algiers balcony
Death you sneering policeman caught red handed

Death you slip through a noose
Death you slipknot *in* a noose

Death you moose looking for breakfast
Death you ripe berry ready to be plucked

Do I believe any of this?
Black door into Someplace?

Tunnel out the living body into a new body
this time with no earth in it

Under the earth Death
Under the eye of the clock Death

Under God's watchful Eye Death
in His breath death His inbreath Death
and His outbreath Death

We are right there at the punch line
we've made the ball of light in the air
with our hands and
set it rolling

We are merrily along
hoping for the best death

Owl eye skunk drunk Death
punch drunk puckered over with Kiss of Death

Smack!

Like *this*
Death!

2/1

55 GRAND CENTRAL STATION

A single fly saw God through its
fly's eye and

saved the world

A single snowflake charted the
dimensions of heaven

and Grace descended

A single heartbeat in all of us
hit a note of wonder

and silenced thunder

Neither addition nor subtraction
makes a modicum of difference

in the ultimate equation

Allah's Oneness is His Wholeness
and His Wholeness is His

Grand Central Station

2/2

56 AT SEA

The navigator struck his head
and the ship foundered

After the storm abated
they lost their bearings

In calm green waters
far from any island

A week later
the stores began to dwindle

The night sky dazzled
with its trillions of stars

The day's drab sunlight
blinded them with its glare

No one died
but they could feel death approaching

A pod of whales
was sighted in the distance

It grew closer
until the ship was surrounded

The snuffing and snorting could be heard
and the spray of spouting

Some could catch glimpses of their eyes
as they saw they were being watched

By these tons of different creatures
dark slick bulks in the water

The sun shone yellow
through oceanic mist

They felt the boat
slowly being propelled

They could hear the hissing of escaped air
as if out elephant trunks

The whales were indifferent creatures
to their human communication

Arguments on board
as to whether they should slay one and eat it

Reason prevailed
as they'd have no way to retrieve it

They could feel the boat
move steadily through the water

Their arguments concluded
when they sighted a sliver of island

As it approached
the shuddering subsided

The dark noisy bulks in the water
disappeared one by one

The Hand of God
left its imprint on their hearts

They left off feeling
alone in the universe

In a few hours
they'll quietly reach dry land

One baby was born on board
one lady died

Every year since then
they meet and embrace each other

Every year since then
they wonder at what happened

The cause of their good fortune
is the source of their wonder

Your salvation
sits beside you

Your salvation
is within you

2/4

57 WATERFALL

The stable dog howls at the slightest sound
but our hard hearts lock at a sigh

Ants shift their trail when the wind shifts
but we intrepidly muck on

At a cruel word a young boy recoils inside
but the cruel world has frozen it for use

There's a science to listening and hearing and seeing
an art to surrender to enable us to be

within the waterfall pummeled by His Grace
instead of just feeling its spray on our face

2/6

58 ENOUGH TINY STONES

Enough tiny stones piled on
top of each other make a

Himalaya

Enough tiny drops gathered in a
big enough basin make an

Atlantic Ocean

Enough of our heartbeats hitting the gong of
God's uttermost Oneness in a

glade of singing trees and hovering
rain clouds make a

congeneity with His Unity

and each speck in the universe
becomes a mirror for His

Face

in pure space

and we are taken

from our place

59 WINDOWS

In a filled window
you can't see out

In an empty window
everything's clear

2/7

60 LITTLE SPOTLIGHT

A little spotlight turns on somewhere
in the universe

A rootlet green as emerald
twists out of it and down

into fertile space

And from it a tree spreads tall
shadowy branches into blackness

filled with incandescent creatures
and rung round in coils with
incandescent birds in

incessant flight

And in the heart of that spotlight and
pulsating throughout its branchings

Allah's Name broken into zillions of
tiny names and reformed into

One Name both vast and dimensionless with
quadrillions of repetitions His golden
Name now echoing through our heartbeats

somewhere in the universe

where a little spotlight turns on

sitting on the side of my bed

writing this down

2/8

61 THE ULTIMATE POEM

I don't know why

but I think the ultimate poem
would have the sleekness of a horse
and the sound of the sea

and a way of seeming to disappear occasionally
and rise to an unreachable height
while sounding the lowest notes on the
linguistic register simultaneously

and be both body and soul
while whistling with a kind of
crystalline clarity

going off on a thunder and
back on a lightning bolt

and singing slightly off key
while yet enunciating perfectly

catching the whole cosmos in
one wink

gorgeously
its whole array of
stars and planets

enough to dazzle us bewilderingly

with the sleekness of a horse
and the sound of the sea

2/13

62 TRAIN TO BALTIMORE

We're heading to Baltimore
where Edgar Allen Poe lies
deep and anonymous

his last imprecations perhaps
still ringing through the streets
against the billion bricks

We're heading to Baltimore by train
along the backs of cities
where old metal machinery is stacked
and empty warehouses blink into the
fog

The train's gotten very slow
perhaps giant angels have
wrapped its cars in huge canvas
wings to slow it down

Out the window
scrap metal and parked cars

Do I catch a glimpse of Paradise
through the clouds?

Or is it here
in the rumble of steel wheels against
tracks?

The whole world's gone white
except for some skeletal
black trees

Towering tapered brick smokestacks
against the sky

A few slack red windsocks
in the mist

2/12

63 A VERY BLUE PIRATE

A very blue pirate lamented that he'd
gone astray

*"Where did I go wrong that I thought
the world's oyster was mine
for the taking*

*and if no pearl was found inside
I could lay waste to the oyster-bed?"*

He was a unique pirate for sure
with such awareness

He swung way out on the yardarm
and watched the sea below him

turbulently churning

"Like my world" he thought
"folded in chaos"

What monsters of the deep
lurked in its watery closets?

What hand could come out
and drag him down?

And then he saw the dawn
God's watercolors pink the sky

The land he left
and the land he would never see

The gallows waiting for him
on a lone hill

And he dove into the sky
in his heart

and disappeared from sight
into interior night

2/13
(written on train from
Baltimore to Philadelphia)

64 PEWTER MOONLIGHT

Old men are writing poems
by pewter moonlight

They live in different parts of the world
but their pen unites them

Their blood is as thin as rivers
after winter floods and the
springtime dries them

Each of them writes his ode
to pewter moonlight

Their eyes ache from peering deep
into lamplight

They've seen the comings and goings
and sheep led to slaughter

The night no longer holds any
terrors for them

One ray of moonlight from the window
is enough to save them

The Holocaust is over and slavery and
cries of despair

New chains are on their way
with clanking regularity

Humankind often finds its better angels
disposable

Old men are writing poems
on rickety tables

Chrysanthemums wither in the
vases before they are done

Everything in reality takes place
by pewter moonlight

The sound of their pen scratch
is enough to heal the world

2/15

65 THE HORSES IN MY POEMS

"There'll be no more horses in my poems"
he said and one
galloped through anyway

*"The extension bridge shall not extend
any further than it needs to"* he affirmed
and with a groan the metal expanded

*"If these bubbles would just stay suspended in the
air for a few moments longer"* he sighed
as they all burst around him

The cat that leapt to the ground
just leapt back to the ledge

The chanteuse who lost her voice backstage
just found it again
as she walked out front

The horse that galloped friskily through this
poem neighed and bounded over the
far horizon and was gone

Things happen as they will by God's will
and we see them that way
either willingly or unwillingly as they are

while the ocean of wisdom continues to stick out its
tongue at the shore

and the shore continues to lick its
lips and kiss the froth

under cover of darkness
or naked in broad daylight

2/19

66 GOD'S HEADY CUPS

Drinking freely from God's heady cups
that's the life for me

The various entrances in the air
God's given us to enter by

at any time or place
heartbeat keyhole remembrance the key

to absolute floating contingency
with His near company

Take your hardscrabble labyrinthine
political assailants
far from me

and pass the heady wine to be an
inebriate utterly

Passing by wise ones in His Garden
on their way to nowhere in particular

with godly cordiality

whose hearts converse the way clouds
pass in the night sky invisibly

whose words ignite the worlds with
His true divinity

2/19

67 THE COKE-BOTTLE BOTTOMED BOAT

The coke-bottle bottomed boat
through which he looked

showed him underwater galaxies passing
in slow majesty

Great fins like great fans moved in
processions like victorious flags

Long wriggling arms and legs of gelatinous
thinking entities crawled up the water rushes
as if up glass

Beady eyed seemingly nearly dead beasts
slid forward without skipping a beat

Sky with murky clouds appeared as if
upside-down here undersea where
no sun shone

All is indelibly Allah in every realm
seen in slow motion here and as if all
color drained

How much ocean fits in the
bead of a drop?

In a tear in the corner of your eye
could an ocean reside?

The Face of the Lord on the
face of the waters

I weep for a world that
never leans underwater

I go to sleep now in that realm
with my eyes wide open

God bless me with the oxygen I need
to complete my journey

2/20

68 TIME TO ASSESS THE UNASSESSABLE

Time to assess the unassessable
and calculate the incalculable

turn the tables on the unturnable
and shift the focus on the unshiftable

The snouts of unknown fish are appearing
for the first time above the surface

and the bubbles they blow are full of
indescribable worlds

Fantastic palaces and extended gardens
afloat in a pristine blue air

with rainbows crisscrossing behind them
and the music of unactivated fingers

on vibrationless strings
now not even needing sound waves

to enter our hearts

The world has effectively come to an end
and begun again

Only the unasleep noticed its passing
and its reassembling in a

new nature
whose trees shed no leaves but light

and whose light falls like leaves
from a height

accessible by all

2/22

69 CHEMICAL MAKEUP

Hydrogen carbonate and helium tetrachloride –
Combined together could they

produce a man?
Once mortal we seem to think mortality's easy

and the life of a frog in a green pond
too far beneath us

The zillion wheels awhirl in the machinery of night
can't produce the happiness available

to a mortal on this earth whose milk mustache
sits above grateful lips and celebratory vocal chords

We walk on this round ball as if
it belonged to us

Ask the Apaches to whom the earth belongs
having had their small portion pulled out

from under them
and replaced with a cubicle

locked from the outside
Or ask the birds of the air

who see it pass below them as they fly
and clouds cross over it

covering its features with mist
Or ask the earthworm

who only owns its wriggling length
as it wallows blindly through its muddy portion

The heads of all of us should be
removed and replaced with lamps

for all the light most of them shed
instead of more reliable filaments

The hearts of all of us should be removed
and replaced with open plains and

rolling prairies for all the vastness they
contain when God Himself says

nowhere else in the entire
universe contains Him once we

hold Him most dear
Our mortal bodies will be removed soon enough

and all the good they're capable of
curtailed when one gesture is enough

to insure us closeness to Him and one gesture is enough
to banish us forever from His Grace

2/24

70 UNFATHOMABLE DEPTHS

"Three beatings were all it took
before I received the Light of the Lord"

one convict said

Another spoke about the blackness of crows
and how some reach iridescent purple

Another seemed to take flight over
a bridge of hope and water

while a fourth walked in a single circle all day
until he found release

The patchwork of light and dark
is a covering over all

We go out through an indication
not quite true north or south

but always under an ocean of stars

In the small skylight of our prisons
a face often appears

One glance is enough to burn away
all our anguish

And if we carry that face around with us
all it sees and all who see it

are alleviated spectrums in a

widening radius of light as well
as the sound of a waterfall

plunging to unfathomable depths

2/25

71 BROWNIAN MOTION

Something with lids on the ground
that things pop out of

High hoppers like slim kangaroos
or stick figures on pogo sticks

The place needs to be jumping
a generous jiggle of elements

We're going in for a closer look
We're going in for the kill

The brilliant ultra-bright silver knife of
acumen and deep understanding

is needed here
for the phenomena of this world may disappear

while this quest is underway
and the Brownian Motion of atoms is required

to complete the utter tranquility
our souls must maintain for the ultimate delving

into darkness then darker darkness and beyond
with the pull and clank of the machinery of night

coming to a standstill around us
as we swim vertically without moving

into realms where eyes are no longer needed
but innermost ears within ears must open like

newly bloomed flowers of Paradise to pick up the
signals rampant here

their long bronzish finger-like petals
peeling back in God's near sunlight

to let us hear the high pure sound
the only sound left when all other

sound disappears and all our
sight becomes heart's glance into

God's eyes direct

2/26

72 SILVERY RADIANT SONG

Suppose we start with what's right in
front of us

Piles of books and a blue thermos full of
water

How can we reach from this to a
medieval ship on the high seas full of

levitating saints whose vestments
flap like clouds

or salt flats from the wastes of
Africa where the sea once stood

on all fours like a lowing animal
but sank into the sand at last

leaving only its crystally salt skin behind?

Or how to reach from this place to

a simultaneous multiplicity of places
each with its particular

flag and its own coral lagoon
with soft music wafting through swaying

palm trees?

How do we get from where we
are to where we aren't?

From our circumscribed mortal being to
full flight before God's endlessly

Beneficent Face beyond all clouds and
hills all conflagrations and sweet

resolutions of both conflict and
harmony where only choirs inside

grass blades clods and eyelashes can be
heard ascending scales of

jubilant praise?

Our mortality can't define us
but our divine contract can

whose heartbeats constantly sign on the
dotted line before His Majesty

at the beginning not only of our own
short lives but also at the beginning point of the

earliest millennia of shade and
light across earth's billowing waters

where levitating saints whose vestments
flap like clouds float now on waves of

silvery radiant song

2/27

73 FOUR GARDENS

Everything's velvety dark and
warm furry and fuzzy in its

particulars each new vista or room full of
people or not empty or crowded with a

large polished grand piano silent in the
middle and four huge windows on the

four walls looking out into gardens each
one of which is different

One Oriental with a humped bridge over
purply lotus pools

One thickly brushy and undergrowthy
with toucans clacking huge
bills full of red berries

One plain and cactusy all silvery and
cobalt and turquoisey bluish

And one exclusively roses of all
shades hues and shapes exploding
riotous color

And at the sight of each garden someone
plays a sonata mazurka or waltz on the piano

and the plants come alive and showers
arrive from both above and below to

irrigate our hearts so in need of
God's waters

2/29

74 AFFLUENCE

And one rose in particular
(*yes we're back to the rose motif*)

stood out from the rest
arose from the ashes of the Phoenix

or better yet the National Turkey
reconstituting from the ashy dust

into now a spectacular model city of
rosy hue aglow with dawn's

special gilding and both
arising and opening its petals

domes thoroughfares and at the
precise epicenter a heavenly mosque

meaning not only scrumptiously beautiful
but also interconnecting lower and higher

domains and dimensions making it that much
easier to know that our fervent

prayers are leaving us and rising as they
should out of the sulfurous earthly

air into rarer atmospheres purified as
if through filters for therefore

clearer interpretation though
He Who interprets is also He Who

first inspired their original efflorescence
now risen above the usual level

on a flowing green stem of
affluence

2/29

75 WHEN YOU PAINT THE EYES

When you paint the eyes
don't forget to put little

dots of light in each pupil
to make them come alive

Black islands in those iris discs of brown
blue green or almost golden on

seas of white eyeballs the way
earth floats on greater sky

and is how we see both
it and ourselves

able at any moment to be
turned inside out so that we

see into ourselves from outside or
All-Seeing Reality sees from Himself into our

tiny pools of dimensionless sight
blind except for *His* Seeing

3/1

76 TINY GIRAFFE

A little giraffe the size of a
tweezers loped across the blank

page of my notebook as I wrote this
poem in that endearing scissory

way giraffes lope with their teetering shadows

Of course this didn't really happen
but what a delightful image if it

should have and somehow has
Its reality now in a sweet memory of

imagined movement across this page

O look! A whole herd of them
sweeping across this blue-lined papery

desert now diminishing in size as they
gallop until one by one there are

none at all

3/1

77 TUMBLING IS ONE WAY TO GO

Tumbling is one way to go about the world
or a giant Ferris Wheel for great

overviews and submission to the way things
rise and fall in predictable cycles

or blasting right into the midst of or
creeping around the edges of everything

Sitting very still though maybe not
perfectly still but anyway still enough

are all possible tactics for our mortal
mobility through the various landscapes

in which we find ourselves or
run up against since we can't

just fly either over them or away from them
and burrowing under them is generally impossible

the mountains too high the oceans too low
and one degree at least of

vibratory self-esteem won't let us
admit total defeat

How do we let ourselves go like kites
into the wind but with strong twine

How do we stand and walk into the
utterly transparent cavalcade of things

with ablaze heart forefront and mind firmly at the
wheel

And Allah on our tongues and in our
eyes between

small individual us

and all multiplicity else?

3/3

78 ANGEL OF DEATH

for Shaykh Harun Faye

The angel of death from the time of its creation
has never smiled

It only answered the greeting of the
Prophet Muhammad in the seventh heaven

As if made of stone its stony eyes
stare straight ahead

What wings does it have wings within wings
it holds to its sides?

What glory does it have deep in its
interior vaults it keeps well hid?

God demanded it return the Prophet's greeting
so it did so with deference

What a statuesque Easter Island attitude it has
haughtily looking out to sea

sea upon sea of humanity ebbing and flowing
on an endless surf of becoming and

dying away

What a pivotal point in the cosmic
continuum across galactic rooms

with the shades drawn down

It folds its enormous wings around itself
like a bat right-side up

It holds the entire world in its
black hand like a coin

When a leaf falls from the tree under God's Throne
the person whose name is on it dies

The angel of death has only to read it
on silent lips to make it so

Black horses gallop along the ocean line
turning into swift aquatic birds

then into smoke wisps
then into nothing at all

and our souls take on a sparkling reality in a
new space untempered by

heat or cold

in dazzling new bodies of purity
blinding to the eyes

3/5

79 SLEEPER

In this train going to Baltimore
a young man in white shirt and tie
black shoes and suit pants is

curled up on his seat trying to sleep
head on hand
feet wrenched awkwardly up against the
train wall

as the landscape of wintry trees
whizzes by the window

And he's probably on his way to Washington D.C.
trying to rest before a crucial presentation

with his feet angled crookedly on the armrest
and his legs bent and head on his
folded suit jacket cramped inside his tailored
fabric shell

as the jostly train squeaks and squeals
southbound toward Baltimore

3/5

80 EVERYONE'S EROTIC LIFE

Everyone's erotic life
is something of a mystery to

everyone else

and probably better
left that way

3/5

81 WHEN THE PROPHET CAME IN

We were sometimes noble sometimes venal
sometimes generous sometimes murderous

When the Prophet came in in his
usual way and sat down among us

His elegant brilliance never ceased to amaze us
and the fact that he knew what we
didn't know we needed to know

When the Prophet came in in his
usual way and sat down among us

We'd give up our lives for what he told us was true
while those of the rest of us kept
silent in his presence

When the Prophet came in in his
usual way and sat down among us

We might not have believed him
if not for the Qur'an which
made the material world immaterial and the
spiritual world real

When the Prophet came in in his
usual way and sat down among us

We who knew him before knew he was
telling the truth

when we saw the light that always went
with him

When the Prophet came in in his
usual way and sat down among us

The dust from his robes glittered like starlight
and his face in its brightness shone like the full moon

When the Prophet came in in his
usual way and sat down among us

And his resonant voice in its even
melodious tones had a jewel-like beauty
all of its own

When the Prophet came in in his
usual way and sat down among us

And if ever you were able to look in his eyes
and though he was shy he never
averted his gaze

When the Prophet came in in his
usual way and sat down among us

you might see Paradise in their dazzling light
as well as hear it in the words from his lips

When the Prophet came in in his
usual way and sat down among us

And we felt we were wrapped in wings of angels
and a few feet off the ground

When the Prophet came in in his
usual way and sat down among us

and everyone of us felt suddenly wiser
listening intently to the depths of
what he was saying

When the Prophet came in in his
usual way and sat down among us

and all of us felt we partook of his beauty
his strength and purpose and above all
the Presence of God

When the Prophet came in in his
usual way and sat down among us

To sit in his presence was to sit in the Presence of
God all around and within us
now and forever

When the Prophet came in in his
usual way and sat down among us

and we took that realization with us
wherever we went and whenever we
remembered

how the Prophet came in in his
usual way and sat down among us

and to this day and to this moment I can
see him and feel his totally
humble but majestic presence

when the Prophet came in in his
usual way and sat down among us

It will never end till the end of time and
beyond time just as at the beginning
at the radiant creation's inception

when by Allah the Prophet came in in his
usual way and sat down among us

each and every one of us in
whatever state or station we
happen to be in

for the Prophet to come in in his
usual way and sit down among us

in spiritual presence and eternal
resonance glorifying that pivotal
moment in human history

when the Prophet Muhammad peace be upon him
came in in his usual way with no
pomp but in utter humanity

and sat down among us

3/11

82 WHITE DIAMONDS BLUE DIAMONDS

White diamonds blue diamonds diamonds of all
colors fall in a tempest out of the Unseen

and enter our realm as pebbles and
stones on a forest path that winds

nowhere in particular but leads you
denser into the forest

your feet finding purchase among the
shabby looking stones you even

stoop at one point and pick up a
handful you throw idly into the trees

How can we know the edges and protrusions
of that world into this in their

cunning disguises to not overwhelm us?
Yet glimpsing in a light ray or glint of shine

the beauty to come? The way
creatures look at us before bounding away

The way we look at each other

3/14

83 LINE UPON WAKING FROM A NAP

I feel like a piece of peeled fruit

3/14

84 ANY TRULY SERIOUS ATTEMPT

Any truly serious attempt to get
out of here must be accompanied

by an instruction manual by someone
on the outside either smuggled in or

transmitted through a long line of
successful escapees

We may be able to dig a hole or
fashion keys out of wood but it's a

long shot and we don't really even
know what's out there just a

few feet away
It could be more walls even

higher and deeper than these
and any suggestions however alluring by someone

from the inside alone in exactly the same

situation as we are is likely to fail without
those clear instructions

But see the clouds and hear the crickets!

We must escape

3/15

85 A LITTLE DOOR

A little door at the bottom of it all
opens up and when you

crouch down to get in
it's as vast as the sky itself

You can pick out the stars by night
and the planets by day

Get up from your crouch and
extend throughout all its heavenly spheres

where nothing is really holding us back
except ourselves and a few tall

mountains of bone and lead and
mournful voices

OK they don't exist either

3/18

86 A PLEASURE BOAT

A pleasure boat went sailing
on the back of a young grenadier

who swam just below the surface
and breathed through a kind of sphere

that allowed him to drift down the river
as nonchalantly as dust

though above him on board the skiff
some conversation about *unjust* or *just*

was being hotly argued by the passengers
though the grenadier couldn't know

in his utilitarian position
where the argument would go

For if *unjust* he'd have to be hauled up
and put on the boat with the others

and then treated by them as one of their
either cousins or nephews or brothers

for God's sake and not like a lowly propulsion machine
doomed to swim upstream or downstream

chopping the waters with his breast strokes
in order to accommodate well-dressed folks

3/19

87 WHAT IT'S LIKE TO BE A DUCK

The ducks descend in orderly lines
and skid to a stop in the water

It's not me who's made it so
but absolute duckness fashioned out of thin air

Their wings extended and feet straight out for landing
and we can only surmise how they measure their descent

they see with an airline pilot's accuracy
by their sweet genius or else they'd crash into trees

Lovely ducks of total innocence and floatability
as well as perfection in their nosedives

They swim along as nobly as kings
then go nose down and rump up in the water

then back up again as nobly as before
though I have no idea what it's like

to be a duck

3/21

88 GULP

Everything all at once takes a pause
then resumes again

We can't see or feel it most times
a crack the size of the cosmos

sealed up in an illusion of continuous flow
a pause between one breath and the next

that includes every star no matter
how far away and every sun long

beyond eye- ear- or any-shot
a gulp that isn't quite a

gulp or a blink that doesn't mean a
moment exactly of darkness

so infinitesimal a break no worm
or wombat feels anything at all

But what could heave itself
between one living existence and the next is so

monumentally gigantic so beyond any
conception of infinitude

And there and on both and all sides
is Allah and there He on all sides also *isn't*

O sweet Mercy O sweet rain of
elements sweet God of it all

That we exist at all O God
in this rush!

3/14

89 LITTLE SAUCY JOHNNY

Little saucy Johnny
talked about the world to come

No one would believe him
Little saucy Johnny

One by one they died
Saw what was before them

Saw the doors and archways
trees of flame trees of ice

Saw the pit the starry wheel
golden rivers milk and honey

Saw the charging snorters
heard the quiet singing

Little saucy Johnny
turns out knew a thing or two

Resting in his grave
Little saucy Johnny

Heard the distant mountain
saw the parting water

Went to where he went to
Little saucy Johnny

3/26

90 CREATURE QUINTET

The purplest peacock you ever saw
and the reddest rooster

and the pinkest pig and the yellowest
giraffe and most zigzag zebra

got together one day in the most
unlikely convocation on this good earth

and sang five-part harmony
in order to divert our attention from

the true import of their
impersonation of zoo animals in a

slightly exotic version of Animal Farm
and they whispered in the

universal mammalian and avian
language of their hopes and desires

their aspirations as much as their
fervent appreciation for where they had

gotten to and to Whom Who'd
gotten them there

There arose a dust cloud
so they stepped within it and howled

and when the dust cloud had passed
our quintet was gone

getting down to some serious business
in Poughkeepsie or Detroit

4/2

91 FIND YOUR WAY

You can find your way by the light
of the moon or a total stranger

Each tree in the dense forest
is its own kingdom

The map you have in the palm of your
hand is map enough

The light of dawn is a reminder to
keep in the back of your mind

We come this way only once and
must interpret the signs

and that all of the signs have been
sent by the Sign Sender

Who watches over us from birth to
death and Who sees us

That we walk in the Light of that
gaze and become at home in it

We can take a break in the
sequence of things but there is no break

We can't see to the end of the
road until we're on it

The stag lowers his antlers and
Paradise shines in the dark

The air hovers within itself and
the night lifts its heavenly slates

The writing everywhere becomes materiality and
the reading of it becomes immateriality again

He Who has sent it all waits for us
to acknowledge His Presence

Our feeble eyes can barely make out
shadows in the dark

When the sun comes up on the other side
all becomes clear

In our heartbeats is the syncopation that
draws us forward and the Braille to read by

In the center where the light is
the mountain shows its height

We've come a long way from the beginning
and the end is near

The singing in the air all around us
is what will get us there

And the dawn prayer

4/6

92 START THE CYCLE

Start the cycle at the drop of silver
that lands on your tongue

Its dazzle lights up the caves of our hearts
arrayed along a line from pole to pole

Don't let distraction for a moment divert you
from the mirror of the sky through which

those who would travel nearer
gaze past their own being into His dimensionless

non-being Whose outspread arms
have created the world

in a never-ending simultaneous arising

each face of which speaks His Name
so tenderly within us

I can't even begin to say

Little tiny round black mouse eyes
that see everything they need to see

Our eyes in love's flowering canyons
for His delight eternally

4/10

93 GORGEOUS STARS

for Malika

Saucers of light *my God!* what about
the other place settings?

Why not flying plates or
even sky-borne place mats?

And who might sit down at the
table of all this celestial clatter?

The sky becomes our tablecloth
as we navigate with fork and spoon

And the butter knife the sleek
silver ship through star after star

Until we land again right in
front of us where the meal will be

And the moon comes out and it's
my wife with another culinary exploration

worthy of the entire NASA budget
enough to invite extraterrestrials with the

twirling odors and scrumptious flavors
and the way she bends over the table

to serve
like a nameable constellation of

gorgeous stars

4/10

94 SPECKS

The specks on a dot at the
bottom of a tiny blip

are not without space enough
for a planet like Mars to fit

with enough space around it
for oceans of stars to swim

and catapult at once
to where everywhere is neat and trim

with haunting song echoing
through all starry atmospheres

and sweet music to circulate
from hidden celestial gears

somewhere in all of this

And there are millions of these tiny specks

and each has more than this allows
as each makes its lifelong trek

from origin to origin
with nothingness in between

where only God is nothing else
remaining perfectly serene

creating and destroying with
utter love and deep concern

that each speck in the universe
take a breath and have its turn

4/11

95 THE RIPPLES SHIMMER SILVER

The first step is to remove the self
and if you've done that the lesson is over

Or next the waterlogged ponies that
always seem to nervously precede you

Or next those silver ribbons in the sky hanging just
above eye level which distract you

And then those bridges – get rid of them
they go nowhere

Down to the bone down to the dusty plain
the wind howls there for its own amusement

Ants are the lions of this place
the wind ruffling their manes

No one said this would be easy
Are you still exactly the same?

Have we come this far and you
still bring that inflatable doll?

The night is a lethal spider –
one bite and we're gone!

Nothing between us now
and the real thing

God's the whiteness that blows across
as well as all the rest

Don't worry now if you're any different

By His Mercy we're there and it's
all done for us down to the tiniest detail

And those squeaky dolphins leaping
over and under each other at sea

and the moon's out and its
ripples shimmer silver

4/13

96 ENTERING THE NIGHT

Entering the night as one
enters high adventure

The anchorite at prayer
whole vistas opening before him

endless ripplings of white horses
pounding surf on a beach

Light everywhere as pewter as possible
glinting off leaves and stones

The heart on its punctual mission
with its beats and its in-between beats

To enter new places with
nothing new about them

Earthly screams are gone and the
earth is folded like a fan

or hands in prayer
as silent as space

No eyes see the same
yet all eyes are alike

Who but ourselves
awaits us up ahead?

And the air that surrounds it all
touched with His subtlest song

4/14

97 THE NEXT STEP

Loaves into fishes

Then into fishermen

4/15

98 THE GROUND WE STEP ON

The song we heard over the fence
was the world turned upside-down

to this one

And the oceans blinked and all was
washed clean

And the clouds opened their fluffy lips
and out floated words birds

flew through soaring on their updrafts

The nickels and dimes of these household trees
shed their leaves in our pockets

and fall through our eyes to the
ground we step on

4/16

99 THE CLOCK ON THE BARK

The clock on the bark showed forty days
and the animals knew it would soon be over

But nothing in the turbulent waves and sky
gave any indication the decree was fulfilled

In the midst of the mist only mist was visible
neither land of beginning nor land of the end

The crows were silent and the donkeys courteous
You could hear straw rustle and the slap of water

The human family huddled together
squinting to get at least a glimpse of the beyond

Though Noah was calm to the core and certain
God's watery map was as clear as if drawn

He stood in his rough-sewn clothes with the others
though invisible prophetic robes glowed gold

At the absolute inception of the Truth he knew
how safe the boat was soon to become

And soon it perched on a stable mountaintop
crest of an earth-wave coming to rest

And they streamed out comfortably to the
rest of our days in pairs and species

to the end of time

4/18

100 THE ONLY REAL LIFE

The only real life is the soul life
say what you will

The only real world is the next world
we'll soon know

The bicycles of the sky disperse into
cloudy drifts

their spokes farther and farther apart

The famous hills and dales of
the earth fall and rise rise and

fall

throwing up snowmen and fire demons
in their congenial upheavals

Once one footing's established
the rug is pulled the bridge

cranked to the side into shadow

The only true sun is not this sun
blazing contentedly though it

warm vegetation to feed and clothe us
season after season

Past the blues and greens
other blues and greens more

vividly ablaze await us

And the cool drink that allays our
thirst complete and is passed around

God's pin drops to earth through the sky
and lands point first

exactly where we are
moving or still

and the pinprick and the ache
are His glory in its purest form

4/22

101 OUT THE AIRPLANE WINDOW

Looking out the airplane window
at scribbly ribbons of water

Patches of green against brown
and long loops of rivers way below

suddenly flashing strings of silver
then puff clouds like delicious fantasy lands arising

from the mist horizon above our eminently
habitable planet we've lived on and

sometimes squandered sometimes honored

Then out the window again *(above Mosul!)*
at so few human conglomerations after all

Yet so much mayhem down there
as this plane above it all like a loud and

continuous exhalation
churns by

4/23

A line about to explode into roses
a song about to explode into breaching whales

The horizon's filled with them mingling
with fishing boats in moonlight

A thought from the heart about to explode
into a plain as far as the eye can see

lined with diminishing telephone poles
and vultures scavenging what they can

from our excessive detritus

A bowl about to explode into the
sea itself with all its serpents

A body about to explode in a lithe and
silvery essence writhing gracefully over the sky

An end about to explode into a
beginning and a beginning to zoom ahead

to an end wreathed in the roses of the
first line as well as leaping invisible beings

Everything on the verge of becoming either
something else nothing at all or most

deeply and simply what it is itself but
constantly on the verge nevertheless

And sleep about to explode into
avenues of direct instruction from the Unseen

And our hearts about to explode once and for all
into those quiet tabernacular receptacles capable

of hearing The Voice that brings peace to all
as well as transmitting it in words and

delectable silences

And those silences about to explode not into sound
but into more tangible and habitable silences

And those silences about to explode into
the diamond roadway to the Presence of God

And that Presence only by itself neither
about to or not about to do or be

anything but all-pervading and
ever present

without cessation
eternal in active stillness

just
it is

4/28

103 TO SLEEP TO DREAM

As a hill turns in to a mountain's cave
so our hearts turn in to the night to sleep

opening out to unsuspected dream landscapes
of graveyards festooned in twirling ribbons of roses

or parades of boisterous revelers who are
themselves both graves *and* roses

in living presences mute in the
awake world but musically vocal in sleep

and remaining in the dark there when we open our
eyes again to morning light

though alive in their own system of
disappearance somewhere perhaps

fully engaged in another world
beyond our making

upon our waking

5/7

104 AS SOON AS THE BLAST IS HEARD

As soon as the blast is heard
or a tiny crowded muffled thud

a rumble under our heels that
pushes things around on the plate shelf

or that cracks pop's spectacles in their case
or on the pinched professor's nose bridge

or that startles horses who canter off
into a ditch amid barking dogs

or strange purplish streaks in the sky
or anything at all unusual overhead

the earth itself straining at its hinges
and the seas aching in their chains

below sewn crisscrosses of gulls
and other water foul screaming far from land

Or it may come in silence with no commotion at all
as grimly as a grave dug in the ground yet unfilled

or as quiet as a cowering mouse when the room light's lit
or nothing at all that distinguishes itself

say in the middle of a trivial conversation
not about elemental or high dimensional things

but about a TV program or a shopping list
or trying to remember a 1940s movie star's name

in a corridor of quiet as stone silent as a
hospital ward at midnight

And as soon as this comes to pass
and we dread the consequences of our actions

for apocalyptic reasons on the
personal as well as cosmic scale

on a still Summer afternoon
or in some hell-broken loose Winter storm

when the house shakes in Beethovianic fury

and we remember the simplicity and the code
to His manifest Presence and Satisfaction

and that no one has real mercy but Allah
given absolute proof by our continued existence

Thud drip or sizzle of no sound at all
heralding both the absolute break into

radiant salvos or the status quo

And it all folds back again into our hearts
like a perfect origami making of them

both receptacle and origin of all things
as well as God's eternal dwelling place

from beat to beat at His perfect pleasure
and in His good time

5/10

105   LOVE BUCKET

The love bucket sways over the abyss
spilling all its contents down below

We're lucky if we get hit

5/12

106 SALMON

I leap these giant salmon falls
like a vertically charging bull

wild eyes wide and blinkless in my
brute determination to get home

though it cost me my life
to bring life to life and the afterlife

and the whole world is doing the same
in my eyes

Look at it urging upward against the
downrush leap after leap its mouth agape

pulsating crouch springing forward
against the eternal wall endlessly ascending

Where's the music to accompany this striving?
Is it the sound of these tons of water against me?

Is that the sweet symphony to my soul?

When I fall back with all my strength
I haven't lost ground so much as

tested the resiliency of my intention
against all odds

Hear the held crescendo's deep chord
in the distance?

The exhausted but victorious serene
and greater knowledge come

in the spent muscle of arrival
the last glad spasm

of success

5/14

107 BUTTERFLY WINGS

Scribble it all out at last
every blood line every grimace and

sigh that strings its doleful bells
along earth's ringing walls

down to where giraffes bend to drink
and in the deeps eyes too dark to see sunlight

so the sky becomes optical
gazing at everything below it with divine vision

If only one voice were to rise above the crowd
proclaiming both victory and defeat for all of us

and its modulations were enough to make
even the most hard-hearted weep

would both whales and angels join in chorus
and would the stones that line the

Prophet's walkways come alive again
in humble salutation?

The profoundest tones of this life
are the most silent and unobtrusive

but under the general planetary racket
their saintly modalities can be heard

with the creaky growing of trees and the
squeaky muscular hatching of butterflies

their wet wings drying in God's sunlight
right on time

5/15

108 OH LORD

Oh Lord these little high-pitched chirps
from one of your lesser birds

No plumage although in my coloring
perhaps I most resemble the English Sparrow

a kind of scruffy nondescript English Sparrow
like the ones that get batted off perches at my feeder

Though Lord you let me fly now and then
in indeterminate sky to an indefinable

somewhere nearer Your location
although it be more by *locution* than location

How these merry words circumscribe
not an essence but perhaps some of the echoing lineaments

of approach while in themselves
in their evanescence

being in passionate love with what they describe
themselves being only linguistic shadows

casting on a wall of space

their invisibly single-most divine Subject
in a reversal of the usual order of things

to get closer and closer to the
living breath that animates all

Now I can hear some of my brighter colleagues
sing the dawn from its black density

to daylight's transparency in which
all things move and have their being

and to whose earthly chorus from time to time
with gratitude

You let me join

5/16

109 THE JOYS OF READING

Reading is the world in miniature
even when it's epic

The great armies of Homer arrayed on the beach
are like ants to us looking down at the page

or even hearing of them recited by oak fire
in the hand-carved lodge in original Greek

Assimilable telescoping down to where
us race of dwarves can take it in

True love or Borneo exploration
without either progeny or mosquitoes

That which is huge in us like real
skirmishes and actual deaths

unthinkable realities in real life
in the slit-eyed contemplation of them

in an inner universe not any less vast
for being interior

now tiny and worthy of the near-sighted
though it put us in God's position

able to see and comprehend the epicness of
all creation from a superior position of seeing or hearing

even that laudable for our souls'
humanness and simpatico bond with all on any scale

Ah there's another fleet of ships gone
exploring past the dragon's oceanic edges

in danger of drop-off

or turn a page and
we're in Paradise!

5/17

110 ROUND SHINY MARBLE

On a round shiny marble
floating in space

lived a round shiny monarch
who thought he'd live forever

He had flocks of geese
who worshipped the ground he walked on

and many died
so he knew he'd outlived them

Clouds in the sky passed in
various shapes or dispersed completely

So he thought he'd be eternal as sky
where things form and disappear

rather than like clouds
insubstantial and volatile as vapor

He gave edicts in front of mirrors
and everyone obeyed them

He strutted and primped
and everyone applauded

He wrote one poem that said
"Hail to ME *who lives forever!"*

But one day he died
slumping into his ermines

The geese flew off in flocks
all the way back to Canada

The mirrors reflected the shifting
clouds and endless blue sky eternally

And the round shiny marble
floated in space without him

much to his surprise

5/18

III HIS PERPENDICULAR THRONE

Love for Allah is a Great Simplicity
while love for all else complexifies redundancy

Of all the horses in a race from the starting line
only one wins who is all the other horses combined

whose confident canter to receive the winning wreath
represents all the other contestants in perfect form

in one toss of mane or flick of tail
as its trillion hooves resound

And when we turn from the race
to Allah Who commands them all

winners and losers disappear
in the swift light of a perfect outcome

Oh face of my single beloved
disappearing around the edges

At the heat center of your graceful animation
is His Light pouring through you

in floods from His perpendicular Throne

5/19

ABOUT THE AUTHOR

Born in 1940 in Oakland, California, Daniel Abdal-Hayy Moore's first book of poems, *Dawn Visions*, was published by Lawrence Ferlinghetti of City Lights Books, San Francisco, in 1964, and the second in 1972, *Burnt Heart/Ode to the War Dead*. He created and directed *The Floating Lotus Magic Opera Company* in Berkeley, California in the late 60s, and presented two major productions, *The Walls Are Running Blood*, and *Bliss Apocalypse*. He became a Sufi Muslim in 1970, performed the Hajj in 1972, and lived and traveled throughout Morocco, Spain, Algeria and Nigeria, landing in California and publishing *The Desert is the Only Way Out*, and *Chronicles of Akhira* in the early 80s (Zilzal Press). Residing in Philadelphia since 1990, in 1996 he published *The Ramadan Sonnets* (Jusoor/City Lights), and in 2002, *The Blind Beekeeper* (Jusoor/Syracuse University Press). He has been the major editor for a number of works, including *The Burdah* of Shaykh Busiri, translated by Shaykh Hamza Yusuf, and the poetry of Palestinian poet, Mahmoud Darwish, translated by Munir Akash. He is also widely published on the worldwide web: *The American Muslim, DeenPort*, and his own website, among others: www. danielmoorepoetry.com. He is also currently poetry editor for *Seasons Journal* and *Islamica Magazine*. *The Ecstatic Exchange Series* is bringing out the extensive body of his poetry in book form (complete list of published works on page 2).

POETIC WORKS BY DANIEL ABDAL-HAYY MOORE
Published and Unpublished

Dawn Visions (published by City Lights, 1964)
Burnt Heart/Ode to the War Dead (published by City Lights, 1972)
This Body of Black Light Gone Through the Diamond (printed by Fred Stone,
      Cambridge, Mass, 1965)
On The Streets at Night Alone (1965?)
All Hail the Surgical Lamp (1967)
States of Amazement (1970)

Abdallah Jones and the Disappearing-Dust Caper (published by The Ecstatic Exchange/
      Crescent Series, 2006)
The Chronicles of Akhira (1981) (published by Zilzal Press with Typoglyphs by Karl
      Kempton, 1986)
Mouloud (1984) (A Zilzal Press chapbook, 1995)
Man is the Crown of Creation (1984)
The Look of the Lion (The Parabolas of Sight) (1984)
The Desert is the Only Way Out (completed 4/21/84) (Zilzal Press chapbook, 1985)
Atomic Dance (1984) (am here books, 1988)
Outlandish Tales (1984)
Awake as Never Before (12/26/84) (Zilzal Press chapbook, 1993)
Glorious Intervals (1/1/85) (Zilzal Press chapbook, ?)
Long Days on Earth/Book I (1/28 – 8/30/85)
Long Days on Earth/Book II (Hayy Ibn Yaqzan)
Long Days on Earth/Book III (1/22/86)
Long Days on Earth/Book IV (1986)
The Ramadan Sonnets (Long Days on Earth/Book V) (5/9 – 6/11/86) (Published by
      Jusoor/City Lights Books, 1996) (Republished as **Ramadan Sonnets** by
      The Ecstatic Exchange, 2005)
Long Days on Earth/Book VI (6-8/30/86)
Holograms (9/4/86 – 3/26/87)
History of the World (The Epic of Man's Survival) (4/7 – 6/18/87)
Exploratory Odes (6/25 – 10/18/87)
The Man at the End of the World (11/11 – 12/10/87)
The Perfect Orchestra (3/30 – 7/25/88)
Fed from Underground Springs (7/30 – 11/23/88)
Ideas of the Heart (11/27/88 – 5/5/89)
New Poems (scattered poems, out of series, from 3/24 – 8/9/89)
Facing Mecca (5/16 – 11/11/89)
A Maddening Disregard for the Passage of Time (11/17/89 – 5/20/90)
The Heart Falls in Love with Visions of Perfection (6/15/90 – 6/2/91)

Like When You Wave at a Train and the Train Hoots Back at You (Farid's Book)
(6/11 – 7/26/91) (Published by The Ecstatic Exchange, 2008)
Orpheus Meets Morpheus (8/1/91– 3/14/92)
The Puzzle (3/21/92 – 8/17/93)
The Greater Vehicle (10/17/93 – 4/30/94)
A Hundred Little 3-D Pictures (5/14/94 – 9/11/95)
The Angel Broadcast (9/29 – 12/17/95)
Mecca/Medina Time-Warp (12/19/95 – 1/6/96) (Published as a Zilzal Press chapbook, 1996)
Miracle Songs for the Millennium (1/20 – 10/16/96)
The Blind Beekeeper (11/15/96 – 5/30/97) (Published 2002 by Jusoor/Syracuse University
     Press)
Chants for the Beauty Feast (6/3 – 10/28/97)
Open Doors (10/29/97 – 5/23/98)
Salt Prayers (5/29 – 10/24/98) (Published by The Ecstatic Exchange, 2005)
Some (10/25/98 – 4/25/99)
Flight to Egypt (5/1 – 5/16/99)
I Imagine a Lion (5/21 – 11/15/99)(Published by The Ecstatic Exchange, 2006)
Millennial Prognostications (11/25/99 – 2/2/2000)
The Book of Infinite Beauty (2/4 – 10/8/2000)
Blood Songs (10/9/2000 – 4/3/2001)
The Music Space (4/10 – 9/16/2001) (Published by The Ecstatic Exchange, 2007)
Where Death Goes (9/20/2001 – 5/1/2002)
The Flame of Transformation Turns to Light (99 Ghazals Written in English) (5/14 –
     8/21/2002) (Published by The Ecstatic Exchange, 2007)
Through Rose-Colored Glasses (7/22/2002 – 1/15/2003) (Published by The Ecstatic
     Exchange, 2008)
Psalms for the Broken-Hearted (1/22 – 5/25/2003) (Published by The Ecstatic Exchange,
     2006)
Hoopoe's Argument (5/27 – 9/18/03)
Love is a Letter Burning in a High Wind (9/21 – 11/6/2003) (Published by The Ecstatic
     Exchange, 2006)
Laughing Buddha/Weeping Sufi (11/7/2003 – 1/10/2004) (Published by The Ecstatic
     Exchange, 2005)
Mars and Beyond (1/20 – 3/29/2004) (Published by The Ecstatic Exchange, 2005)
Underwater Galaxies (4/5 – 7/21/2004) (Published by The Ecstatic Exchange, 2007)
Cooked Oranges (7/23/2004 – 1/24/2005 (Published by The Ecstatic Exchange, 2007)
Holiday from the Perfect Crime (1/25 – 6/11/2005)
Stories Too Fiery to Sing Too Watery to Whisper (6/13 – 10/24/2005)
Coattails of the Saint (10/26/2005 – 5/10/2006) (Published by The Ecstatic Exchange, 2006)
In the Realm of Neither (5/14/2006 – 11/12/06) (Published by The Ecstatic Exchange, 2008)
Invention of the Wheel (11/13/06 – 6/10/07)
The Sound of Geese Over the House (6/15 – 11/4/07)

The Fire Eater's Lunchbreak (11/10/07 – 5/19/08) (Published by The Ecstatic Exchange, 2008)

Sparks Off the Main Strike (5/23/08 –)

www.ingramcontent.com/pod-product-compliance
Lightning Source LLC
Chambersburg PA
CBHW020853090426
42736CB00008B/362